The Way of True Riches

MILO KAUFFMAN

HERALD PRESS
Scottdale, Pennsylvania
Kitchener, Ontario

THE WAY OF TRUE RICHES
Copyright © 1979 by Mennonite Board of Missions,
    Elkhart, Ind. 46514
Published by Herald Press, Scottdale, Pa. 15683
    Released simultaneously in Canada by Herald Press,
    Kitchener, Ont. N2G 4M5
Library of Congress Catalog Card Number: 79-83505
International Standard Book Number: 0-8361-1885-5
Printed in the United States of America
Illustrations and cover art by Elmore Byler
Design: Alice B. Shetler

15 14 13 12 11 10 9 8 7 6 5 4 3 2 1

Distributed overseas by Mennonite Broadcasts, Inc.,
Box 1252, Harrisonburg, Va. 22801

CONTENTS

PREFACE

Followers of Jesus Christ can be found today all over the world. Among these Christians are Mennonites who take their name from Menno Simons, a Frisian Reformer of the sixteenth century.

Until the nineteenth century, most Mennonites were found in Europe and North America. During the twentieth century, however, mission, relief, and service activities have resulted in a worldwide Mennonite fellowship.

One major emphasis of the Mennonites is to practice daily the teachings of Jesus. This book sets forth some of these teachings concerning stewardship.

The Way of True Riches is volume six of the Mennonite Faith Series listed inside the back cover. The author provides insights for anyone wanting to understand the Christian faith in general and Mennonites in particular.

Anyone wanting to study the stewardship theme further may check the references placed at the back of this book.

—J. Allen Brubaker

1

TWO KINDS
OF
RICHES

YEARS ago I read of two young men starting out in life. Each set a goal for himself. One set as his goal riches—he was going to become wealthy. By hook and by crook, he became wealthy. He loved no one, and no one loved him. His only satisfaction was that he was rich. Like the rich fool Jesus told about, before he could enjoy his riches, he was called from this earth. His money did him no good. Others had suffered and died because he stored up riches. Very few people came to his funeral, for he had not earned the respect of his community.

How different the other young man was. He

set as his goal serving others, being a steward of God. He prepared himself for the ministry and accepted the call to serve a church as its pastor. There he fed the flock of God. He baptized young persons coming into the fellowship of the church. He helped young couples establish Christian homes. He comforted those whose loved ones had died. He challenged his young people to enter Christian service as ministers, doctors, nurses, farmers, and leaders in business.

Later this pastor was called to be the president of his denominational college. There he challenged hundreds of young people to dedicate themselves to the service of the Lord and to minister to the needs of people. Though he lived to be an old man, he never had much money. In fact, at times he had hardly enough to meet his daily needs. But when he died, thousands of people came from far and near to attend his funeral and to honor this steward of God, for he had deeply touched their lives. He had made an important contribution to the denomination and to the kingdom of God.

Which of these young men would you be? I hope no one would choose to be the *poor* rich man. Faithfulness in dedicating ourselves and our possessions to the service of God and our fellowmen is most rewarding and satisfying. Living for self and possessions is bound to end in frustration, futility, sorrow, and regret.

God's Plan
From the very beginning God planned that human beings be the caretakers of His earth. He

put every living thing under their control. He trusted Adam and Eve with the Garden of Eden, the very best of His creation.

Then God said,
   "And now we will make human beings;
   they will be like us and resemble us.
   They will have power over the fish, the birds,
      and all animals, domestic and wild, large and small."
So God created human beings, making them to be like himself.
   He created them male and female, blessed them, and said,
      "Have many children, so that your descendants will live all over the earth
      and bring it under their control.
   I am putting you in charge of the fish, the birds,
      and all the wild animals. . . ."
Then . . . God placed the man in the Garden of Eden
   to cultivate it and guard it (Genesis 1:26-28; 2:15, TEV).

In the Old Testament when a great man put his possessions into the care of a servant, he called this man his steward. The position of steward was a worthy one. Such a servant not only had his master's wealth in his hands, but his honor and his future well-being as well.

Examples of Stewards
The story of Abraham in Genesis 24 gives us an example of a steward. The Lord had blessed

Abraham with flocks of sheep, goats, and cattle, with silver and gold, with male and female servants, with camels and donkeys. Abraham put all of this wealth, as well as his future, into the hands of his servant, Eleazer.

When Abraham was old, he asked his servant Eleazer to take a vow that he would choose a wife for his son, Isaac, from relatives in his home country. The servant vowed to obey his master and was given access to his master's wealth to make the journey.

When Eleazer got to Abraham's homeland, God honored his obedience by leading him to Rebekah. She was one of Abraham's relatives and willing to become the wife of Isaac. Abraham's servant proved himself a worthy steward.

In the familiar story of Joseph in Potiphar's house, we read: "Potiphar was pleased with [Joseph] . . . and made him his personal servant; so he put him in charge of his house and everything he owned. . . . Potiphar turned over everything he had to the care of Joseph and did not concern himself with anything except the food he ate." Joseph said of himself: "[Potiphar] . . . has put me in charge of everything he has [except his wife]. I have as much authority in this house as he has" (Genesis 39:4-9, TEV).

We have nothing quite like the position of steward in modern times. Some men have business managers, but few completely turn over all decisions to them.

But God made us His stewards from the beginning. We are given dominion over living things; all of us are earth-keepers.

However, God has given Christians greater privileges and responsibilities. When Jesus was about to ascend into heaven, He said to His disciples: "I have been given all authority in heaven and on earth. Go, then, to all peoples everywhere and make them my disciples" (Matthew 28:18, 19, TEV).

Jesus gave believers greater authority with this greater responsibility. We now have power from above and are now our brothers' keepers in a spiritual way. We speak of this as Christian stewardship.

This book is intended to help us be better earth-keepers or to carry out in a Christian way the work God assigned to men in the beginning. More than that, it is intended to help us see ourselves as stewards in all aspects of life. I hope the book will help us to take seriously our New Testament charge to give ourselves completely to God. Only then can we serve our fellowmen as Christ did.

Paul felt this charge very deeply. He said of his work for God: "This is how one should regard us, as servants of Christ and stewards of the mysteries of God. Moreover it is required of stewards that they be found trustworthy" (1 Corinthians 4:1, 2).

Peter also held this kind of stewardship to be important—"As each has received a gift, employ it for one another, as good stewards of God's varied grace (1 Peter 4:10).

From these verses we notice: First, we are trustees of God's many gifts and sacred truths.

Second, we are to manage or use these gifts for the good of one another. Third, faithfulness is required of stewards.

Some Principles of Stewards

We can discover some basic principles of Christian stewardship from the Old Testament stories we have just read.

First, when we deal with our own possessions, we are dealing with God's possessions.

In Genesis 24:10 we read that "the servant took ten of his master's camels and departed," for all the goods of the master were in his hands. The Lord led the servant to Rebekah. Then, "the servant brought forth jewelry of silver and of gold, and raiment, and gave them to Rebekah; he also gave to her brother and to her mother costly ornaments" (24:53). Now these precious things which the servant gave away were not his. They belonged to Abraham. But as long as the servant was promoting the cause of his master, he had access to the wealth of the master.

Second, as we deal wisely with God's possessions, our own needs are cared for. As long as Joseph had the confidence of his master, he managed the household, the slaves, and the bank account. He had everything that he needed.

Eleazer and Joseph illustrate the kind of relationship that God wants to have with His stewards. He wants to place His vast resources in the hands of His servants who will faithfully use them to promote His cause. He wants to supply every need of His servants as they carry out His purposes.

As God's servants, we are stewards of all that God entrusts to us. Our bodies, minds, abilities, affections, time, and possessions must be managed with the welfare of others and the glory of God in mind. We are stewards of all of life.

God gives special responsibilities to some of His stewards. In the case of Eleazer, his master Abraham sent him on an important mission—to secure a wife for his son, Isaac. Some ministers, some leaders, some businessmen, some others seem called of God to be stewards of God's purposes at special times and places.

A Steward Must Receive

Receiving is as important a part of stewardship as is giving. We must be good stewards in receiving before we can be good stewards in giving. If Eleazer had not agreed to receive his master's wealth into his hand, he would have lost all opportunity to be a part of God's great purpose for Abraham and his children. If Joseph had not also received and faithfully cared for Potiphar's possessions, he would likewise have failed to receive the honors of God's people for all time.

All that we have comes from God. We cannot share love with others except as God's love is shed abroad in our hearts. We can minister to others only as we receive abilities and strength from God. We can give only what He has given to us.

Perhaps our greatest sin is not that we do not give enough, but that we do not receive enough—we are not receptive to His gifts which He longs to entrust to us to share with others. We do not love as we should because we are not open to His love. We do not have victory and power because we have not tapped His great resources. We cannot give freely because we have not received freely. Giving is dependent on receiving. At the same time, receiving is dependent on giving. "Freely ye have received, freely give" is one side of the coin. "Give and it shall be given you" is the other side.

Eleazer, Joseph, Paul, and Peter never doubted that the Master's authority had been given to them to use for His glory. They spoke in His name; they acted as their Master would act. So our words and deeds reflect, likewise, the character of God, our Father.

God's Purpose in Creating Man

Since God gives His resources into the care of His stewards to promote His purposes, it is very important for us to know His purposes. Why did He create the world and you and me?

God, who is a good steward Himself, used His great power to create this wonderful universe. He created a good and beautiful world. Isaiah says that God did not make the world in vain. He created it to be inhabited. To be a good steward of His love, God could not merely bestow it upon Himself. So He created a host of angels to love and share His glory and be His ministering spirits.

After God had created the earth, the vegetation, and the living creatures, He declared, "It is good." But God was not yet satisfied. "There was not a man to till the ground," no caretaker. So

God created man in His own image to be the steward of creation. Man was to multiply and fill the earth. God wanted a multitude of beings made in His image whom He could love and with whom He could share His glory, joy, holiness, power, and wealth. He wanted persons with whom He could fellowship. Man was to be His steward, tilling the ground, dressing the Garden, and subduing the earth. Man was to be God's partner in preparing a community of righteousness, love, joy, peace, and plenty.

What a wonderful world this would be if man had remained a faithful steward of God. In the image of God, man would have portrayed the great attributes of God. He would have received from God, and would have been "filled with the fullness of God." The will of God would have been done on earth as in heaven. Man never would have known war and conflict, poverty and want, sickness and death.

Man's Selfish Failure

But man made a tragic mistake—a fatal choice. Instead of living a life of obedience, trust, and service, he chose instead to disobey God by eating the forbidden fruit. He chose to be his own god instead of serving the Lord. He became self-centered instead of God-centered. As a result of man's choice, he was cursed, as was also the ground and all creation. Man had defiled God's temple. God could no longer dwell in man. The end result was death for the human race.

However, God did not reject man. Instead, He put into action His plan to redeem mankind and to restore the broken relationship. No sooner had man fallen than the Creator became the Redeemer. Jesus, the Lamb slain before the foundation of the world, came and completed this work. God's plan for a community of righteousness, love, and joy did not change. His original purposes will be fulfilled. In the end, the curse of sin will be totally removed. The Tree of Life still exists and is for "the healing of the nations."

After the fall of man and after God put into action His plan of redemption, God's people were no longer merely trustees of creation. They became also God's stewards in reconciliation. God's people in the Old Testament still were stewards of the earth. They also promoted the work of the temple, observed the festivals, gave tithes and offerings, and cared for the needy and oppressed. Further, they were to be God's witnesses among the Gentiles, expressing His holiness, love, and power. Through the centuries, God has been active in His world, teaching, pleading, disciplining, reconciling. "In Christ God was reconciling the world to himself," Paul tells us in 2 Corinthians 5:19.

Our Task Enlarged

Since God was in Christ restoring the world to Himself, our stewardship as Christians becomes much more important. Paul says in 2 Corinthians 5:18, that since God reconciled us unto Himself, He has given us the ministry of reconciliation. Today's English Version says, "God . . . through Christ changed us from enemies into his friends and gave us the task of making others his friends also." As God was making all mankind His friends through Christ, so through His people, His stewards, Christ is reconciling the world.

Man is to be reconciled, but also all of creation—the world—is to be reconciled. When man fell, God's creation fell with Him. It became "subject to vanity," to vainness. It no longer perfectly serves the purposes that God intended. All creation looks forward in hope as illustrated in Romans 8:19-23 (Living Bible).

"For all creation is waiting patiently and hopefully for that future day when God will resurrect his children. For on that day thorns and thistles, sin, death, and decay—the things that overcame the world against its will at God's command— will all disappear, and the world around us will share in the glorious freedom from sin which God's children enjoy.

"For we know that even the things of nature, like animals and plants, suffer in sickness and death as they await this great event. And even we Christians, although we have the Holy Spirit as a foretaste of future glory, also groan to be released from pain and suffering. We, too, wait anxiously for that day when God will give us our full rights as his children, including the new bodies he has promised us—bodies that will never be sick again and will never die."

We Join in God's Purpose

As stewards of God it is our great and glorious privilege to be God's partners in promoting His purposes on earth. We share our testimony of Christ's saving power and we help reconcile men

15

to God. We encourage them to conform to the image of Christ. As ministers of God's peace, we use our time, talents, prayers, and money to help reconcile man to man. We also do what we can to get rid of other results of the fall—disease, poverty, and other enemies of mankind. We use our influence against injustice, oppression, racism, and crime. We conserve our soil, forests, and the natural resources as we have opportunity. We avoid the pollution of the water and air, and the careless use of the earth.

All the efforts of man himself will never bring about a perfect environment. Man himself will never produce a perfect community of righteousness and love. Only our Lord's return can do this. This fact, however, must not keep us from being faithful stewards. We do what we can to make this earth as nearly as possible what God wants it to be. We help persons conform as nearly as possible to the image of Christ.

To accomplish these purposes, as stewards of God, we must first of all be the persons that God wants us to be. We must be filled with the fullness of God—be the temple of God, filled with truth, wisdom, love, joy, holiness, power, and compassion. Not only will we be filled with God, but we will be a channel through which these qualities flow to bless the lives of others.

The True Meaning of Christian Stewardship

What then does Christian stewardship mean? Christian stewardship means receiving God's bounteous gifts, sharing them with others, and using them in promoting the great purposes of

God in the world. The Christian steward recognizes that God is the Owner—"The earth is the Lord's and the fullness thereof." He recognizes that he is not his own, for "you were bought with a price. So glorify God in your body" (1 Corinthians 6:20). The Christian will recognize his dependence upon God, that all he has comes from God. He also recognizes that God does not give him these gifts to be used selfishly, but to be shared and used for the good of the body of Christ.

As we use God's gifts for the good of others and to promote God's kingdom, we are making a good investment—we are using them for our own best interests as well. When we use our time, talents, and possessions selfishly, we do *not* use them wisely. Nor do we get the most out of them for ourselves.

In 1 Corinthians 2:9 Paul, quoting from Isaiah, says, "What no one ever saw or heard, what no one ever thought could happen, is the very thing God prepared for those who love him" (TEV). The joys and rewards of Christian stewardship are beyond man's imagination.

Prayer

Lord, we thank You for the privilege of being Your stewards, partners with You in promoting Your great purposes in the world. May we always be faithful stewards, dedicating our time, talents, and possessions in ministering to others, and in promoting the work of Your kingdom. Amen.

2

ALL OF LIFE
A GIFT

FOR many years a Toba Christian in Argentina
worked faithfully for the government. From his
weekly earnings he was able to buy a brick house.
When he retired on a small government pension,
he used some of the money to buy a little piece of
land. On it he began building a church and later
became its pastor. Near the church he bought
another small piece of land. Then he sold his
brick house. With some of the money, he finished
building the church. Then he built a small stick
house on the land near it so he could minister to
the congregation. As he shares his time, abilities,
and money in service to others, his own life is

enriched, especially during his retirement years.

Life is one of God's gracious gifts to us. If we're grateful for life, we will live in harmony with God's will.

The Apostle Paul teaches us in Romans that we are stewards of all of life. In chapter 12 he challenges us to serve God with our whole being. Because He saved us from sin, we are grateful for His grace and goodness.

We Are Stewards of Our Bodies

Paul tells us to be good stewards of our bodies—"Present them as living sacrifices to God." What wonderful bodies God has given us! We are "fearfully and wonderfully made." The body is capable of doing many things for itself, for others, and for the glory of God. It is the temple of God. It can help minister to the needs of mankind. It can help promote the great work of the kingdom. Our bodies can be instruments of great good if we're good stewards. Paul says, "Know ye not that your body is the temple of the Holy Ghost . . . ye are not your own? . . . Therefore glorify God in your body, and in your spirit, which are God's."

Many people take the attitude, "This is my body. I can do with it what I want. If I wreck it by use of alcohol, drugs, or sin, it is nobody's business." This is a serious mistake. If I willfully misuse my body and harm it in any way, I am not a good steward of it.

What does Paul mean in Romans 6 when he tells us not to yield the members of our bodies "as instruments of sin," but to yield them as "instruments of righteousness to God"? He means we should *not* use our feet to take us to the bar, the gambling den, or other places of evil. We should use them "to go about doing good," as Jesus did. We should *not* use our hands to steal, to accept bribes, to do violence, or to commit sin. We should use them to care for the needs of others and to serve our Lord. We should *not* use our tongues to gossip, lie, or tell immoral stories. We should use them to sing the praises of God and to talk about Jesus and His salvation. We should *not* use our eyes to look upon what is evil, or our ears to listen to what is vulgar and harmful. We should use them to see the needs of the world and to hear the cries of the needy. As good stewards of God we will use the members of our bodies to do good, to help others, and to build up God's kingdom on earth.

Good stewardship of my body means that I keep it healthy and clean. I build as strong and fit a body as possible. I use my body to the glory of God and in the service of my fellowmen. If I unnecessarily harm my body, use it in hurting other people, or use it only for my fleshly pleasure, I am misusing my body and am guilty of bad stewardship. "Therefore glorify God in your body, and in your spirit, which are God's."

We Are Stewards of Our Mental Abilities

Next, Paul tells us that we are to be good stewards of our minds. God gave man great powers when He gave him his mental abilities—the power of memory, the power of imagination, the power of reason and will, the power to create or destroy. Think of what the mind of man has been able to accomplish in technology, in travel, in medical science, in space, and in other ways. We marvel as we think of man walking on the moon, of rockets traveling rapidly toward other planets. The mind of man can be a mighty instrument for good.

How tragic that so often man has not been a good steward in the management of this gift of God! The mind could have, and should have, built a world where war and bloodshed is unknown. Instead it has built a world of conflict. The mind could have, and should have, built a world where poverty is unknown. Instead it has built a world where wealth is in the hands of a few and the masses face starvation. Many keen minds have been more occupied in means of destruction than in meeting the needs of people. Great minds like those of Adolph Hitler and Joseph Stalin and others left the world worse off than they found it because of their greed for power. As a result, millions died in battle. There were millions of widows and orphans. The mind of man, if not used rightly, is capable of destroying the planet earth.

Nations are spending large sums to find new ways to use science. Too often they do this for the power it gives them over other nations, not because of the good the new discovery would do for all people. God never gave us our mental powers to use selfishly or to hurt other people. He expects us to be good stewards in using these powers for the good of others. I once asked some students, "Wouldn't it be too bad if you had to admit that your home would be a better home if you were not a son or daughter in that home? If you had to admit your church would be a better church if you were not a member of it? If you had to admit that this school would be a better school if you were not a student in it? And, at the end of life would have to admit that the world would have been better off if you had never been born?" Paul says we should have "transformed minds." God can change our selfish, violent thoughts to thoughts of peace and good will. Your home then becomes a better home because you are a member of the family. The church becomes a better church because you are a member of it. Your community becomes a better community because you live in it and the world becomes a better world because of your contribution.

With "transformed minds," we become good stewards of these tremendous powers God has entrusted to us. As good stewards of God we will use these gifts for our own good, for the welfare of others, and to promote the great purposes of God.

We Are Stewards of Our Abilities

Paul also tells us that we should be good stewards of our talents. He tells us that each of us is a member of the body of Christ and all of us "members one of another." We are to use our abilities for the good of the body. I like the figure Paul uses here—the church as a body and we as parts of the body. Isn't it wonderful the way the parts and organs of our bodies work together?

When one part is in need or hurt, the other members do what they can to minister to that need. You may be sitting in your living room reading a book. You notice a gnawing in your stomach. Your stomach is calling for food. Your feet and hands could say, "So what, I'm not hurting?" Instead, your feet take you to the cupboard or refrigerator; your hand reaches out and opens the door. Your eyes discover some food. Your saliva begins to flow as your other hand reaches in and picks up the food. Your mouth opens as the hand places the food into it. Then your jaws begin chopping away. All because of the discomfort of a member of the body! Wouldn't it be wonderful if the members of the church worked like that—all seeking to serve the other members?

How miserable or impossible life would be if the organs of our bodies cared only for themselves and failed to cooperate with the other members of the body. So, we as members of Christ must not use our gifts selfishly, but to minister to each other.

It is God who gives our gifts and holds us accountable for their use. The Apostle Peter says, "God has given each of you some special abilities; be sure to use them to help each other, passing on to others God's many kinds of blessings" (1 Peter 4:10, *Living Bible*).

As a good steward of God, if you have musical abilities, you will use them in the music program of your church. If you have the ability to teach, you will be ready to teach in your Bible school. If you have administrative abilities, you should be ready to serve on the church board, or as an officer in the church. If you have the ability to communicate, you will use it to persuade others to become members of the church and the body of Christ. If you have the ability to give, you will give generously to meet the needs of God's people and to promote His work.

A girl who was a good typist went to her pastor and offered to help him prepare the church bulletin and do the correspondence. She was a good steward, using her ability to type to serve her church and her Lord.

God has given us our abilities to minister to others and to promote the work of His kingdom. How tragic when one is entrusted with abilities or possessions and he takes the attitude, "This is mine, I am going to use it for myself." People are in need. God has given him the means to help meet that need, but instead he uses it to satisfy his own selfish desires.

Imagine the hand clutching a bag full of money while the body is starving and crying for food. But the hand says, "This is mine. I won't share it with you." But if the body dies, the hand dies with it, and all is lost. So how could the hand say, "This is mine?" Without the help of the other members of the body, the hand could never have held the money. The eyes discovered it. The feet carried the body to it. The body stooped down so the hand could pick it up. So the money belongs to the whole body. In a similar way, a man could never be rich without the blessings of God and the help of others. What God entrusts to us is for the good of all.

We Are Stewards of Our Affections

In Romans 12 Paul also tells us that we are stewards of our affections and emotions. We are to love what is good and hate what is evil. We are "to be kindly affectioned one to another with brotherly love." The Scriptures also teach that there is a time for anger and a time for rejoicing and sorrow. We are to rejoice with those who rejoice and weep with those who weep.

Some people seem to think that love and joy are good, but that hate and anger are bad. No, each has a rightful place. Without the ability to hate and to become angry, we could not be the persons that God wants us to be. The trouble is that we have not always been good stewards of these feelings or emotions. Too often people hate what they should love and love what they should hate. Instead of loving people, truth, justice, and righteousness, people love money, fame, and sinful pleasures. Instead of hating falsehood, injustice, and things that defile, they hate people of other races who cross their path. How different our world would be if everyone hated sin and injustice and loved truth, righteousness, and justice—loved their neighbors as themselves. The problems that trouble our society, such as hunger and war, would be greatly reduced.

The ability to love and to hate, to be angry and to rejoice are gifts from God. Like other spiritual gifts, they can be used or abused—become a blessing or a curse. Good stewardship demands that we develop and use our affections wisely. We must learn and practice loving what is good, and hating what is wrong. In no area of our lives

is stewardship more important or the results more
rewarding or fateful.

Jesus, Our Example

Jesus, on occasion, displayed anger. His anger
was aroused by attitudes of people that were
wrong and hurtful. William Barclay in his devo-
tional book, *Daily Celebration*, mentions four
things that made Jesus angry.

1. Jesus was angry with anyone who was a hyp-
   ocrite (Matthew 15:7; 22:18; 23:13-29).
2. Jesus was angry with persons who were not
   responsible (Luke 16:19-31; Matthew 25:41-
   46). The rich man's actions did not get him
   into jail, but what he did *not* do got him into
   hell.
3. Jesus was angry with those who loved
   systems—the way things are done—more
   than people (Mark 3:1-6).
4. Jesus' anger was kindled against taking advantage of the poor and helpless (Mark
   11:15-19; John 2:13-17).

We Are Stewards of Our Instincts

God has given us instincts or biological drives
that also demand good stewardship. These include hunger, fear, the desire to possess, social
and parental instincts, sex, and the desire for
relationship with God. William Barclay says in
Daily Celebration that God does not create us
mature persons. We are born with all the instincts or parts we need to build a whole personality, if we follow God's instruction book, the
Bible.

26

Barclay says that if we carefully follow the instructions in developing the parts of our lives, we will develop beautiful manhood or womanhood. If we fail to develop one of these instincts, or overdevelop it, we will have faulty personalities. The instinct of hunger, if properly developed, will help keep us from starving. But wrongly developed, it may result in gluttony or alcoholism. If we ignore the desire to possess, we may develop into spendthrifts, no goods. If we abuse it, we may become misers, thieves, hoarders. If we do not develop the instinct to flee from danger, we may become "daredevils" and die untimely deaths. If we overdevelop it, we may become cowards and this may keep us from performing our duty.

God has given us the sex drive for our good. Without this instinct we could not be the men or women God wants us to be. Rightly used it helps us develop noble manhood, beautiful womanhood. But misused it can result in prostitution, homosexuality, and sex perversions of all types. Wrong sex has wrecked the bodies and lives of multitudes with veneral disease, causing misery and death to thousands. It can break up homes and wreck what could have been happy marriages. Failure to follow God's instruction book in sexual matters can destroy the lives of men and women.

If we obey God's Word in the use of the parental instinct, the result will be a happy home—father and mother loving each other and their children. Children raised according to God's plan are prepared to be good parents themselves. But parents who "do too much for their children" hinder them from growing up and becoming responsible adults.

We are partners with God when we use the instincts of our body to develop strong, Christian personalities and help other persons to do the same. My first responsibility as a steward of God is to develop into the kind of person He wants me to be. Then I can make the greatest contribution to my fellowmen and to the kingdom of God. If I fail to control the desires of my body, I will most certainly fail in other areas—in the stewardship of talents, time, and possessions.

Shining Examples

During a severe famine in Israel there was a poor widow who had only a handful of flour and a little oil left. She was gathering wood to bake the last of her meal into a cake for herself and her son. God told the Prophet Elijah to go to the home of this widow and she would care for him. As she was preparing her last meal, Elijah appeared and asked for some bread. She replied that she had only enough for a cake for herself and her son, then they must die. The prophet told her that if she would first give him some bread, her meal and oil would not fail. Using her last flour, she fed the prophet. True to the word of the prophet, her flour and oil were not exhausted (1 Kings 17:8-16).

By faith this woman was ready to share all she had with the man of God, and found that she had plenty for herself and her son. For many days the three of them had plenty of flour and oil. God's stewards need not hesitate to give out of their poverty when God asks them to do so.

A woman in Santa Rosa, Argentina, experienced God's grace. She told her pastor she wanted to give to help build the church, but had no money. So she asked her husband if she might give her engagement ring in the offering. He agreed, and on a Sunday morning she gave the $300 ring to help build God's kingdom.

Prayer

Thank you, Lord for the bodies, minds, abilities, and powers you have entrusted to us. May we use them wisely as your stewards, ministering to others and promoting your great purposes in the world. Amen.

3

MANAGING
MONEY

A Christian steward puts God rather than money first in life. This means different things for different people according to circumstances. A Toba Christian in Argentina discovered what it meant to put God ahead of money in his life. He owned a number of horses and enjoyed farming his land. However, being a Christian was the important part of his life. One day the Lord spoke to him through a vision in which he was told to go and preach the gospel to the Pilaga tribe. So he sold his farm and went traveling among the Pilaga people. As he preached God's Word, many people responded and began living for God.

Through this Christian's faith and obedience, God was able to bless many other people.

According to the gospels, Jesus says more about possessions than about any other one thing. Why? Because He knew the attitude that men would take toward money. He knew that the love of money would always be a trap for us, capable of leading us to our destruction. On the other hand, Jesus knew that by using money wisely and sharing it, we can be tremendously blessed here and now; we can lay up treasures in heaven for the life to come.

Jesus wanted money to be a source of good rather than harm. However, He knew that if we mismanaged money, we would not be good stewards of spiritual matters.

What the Bible Tells Us About Money

The Bible teaches that God, not man, is the Owner of all things. The silver and gold are His. The cattle are His. "The earth is the Lord's and the fulness thereof, the world and those who dwell therein." God entrusts His creation to man for the good of all who dwell in the earth. Man is the trustee or steward of all material things—all possessions—and is accountable to God for their proper use.

The Scriptures tell us that it is God who gives us the ability to get wealth. Without Him we would have nothing. If God has given us this ability, He holds us accountable for its proper use. Earning money is honorable.

Jesus tells us to make money our servant by sharing it. Money is not our servant when we permit it to become our god. Money is a wonderful servant, but a cruel god. Possessions are not our servants when we use them for getting honor or esteem, or hoard them for ourselves. Money is to be used to help ourselves, to aid our fellowmen, and to bring glory to God.

Jesus warns us not to lay up treasures—or possessions—on the earth, for we will lose them if we do. They should be stored up in heaven where they are safe and will have eternal value. How foolish to earn and save money for this short life only, and so lose it and be poor throughout eternity. We should earnestly covet eternal wealth rather than temporary wealth. We should strive to be rich toward God. This we do by using our money in God-honoring ways.

Another reason Jesus gives for laying up treasures in heaven is that where our treasure is, our heart will be. How true. If I put my money in possessions, I'll worry about thieves. If I put my treasures in houses and land, my heart will be there. On the other hand, if I help to build "the body of Christ," the church, I'll be interested in its welfare. If I help a student go to school, I'll help prepare him to fill a greater place in his community and church. If I help my poorer brother in the church, I'll be more concerned for his entire welfare. If I help send out evangelists, I'll pray that they touch many lives. In short, I'll put my heart in values that last beyond this life.

You can tell where a man's heart is by the way he spends his money. The man who loves alcohol will spend all his money on booze. The person with his heart set on dress will spend much on clothing and jewelry. The young man with his heart set on a bicycle, a motorcycle, or an automobile will put all his efforts toward obtaining one. It is not hard for him to spend his money that way, for his heart is there.

So also, the person who loves the church and its work will give generously to those causes. If I seek first the kingdom of God, my possessions will be available for kingdom purposes (see Matthew 6:19-21).

Some time ago I read the statement, "If you want to know what kind of person you are, look at the stubs of your checkbook. They will tell you." If you have no bank account, consider how you spend your money—whether much or little. How much did you spend selfishly—or even foolishly? How much for luxuries or to gain favor and pleasure? How generously have you shared your possessions with the needy and for the work of the church? God, of course, wants us to have plenty, to enjoy life, and to provide for our family.

Our Lord tells us that it is hard for a rich man to enter the kingdom. This is another reason Jesus was so much concerned about money and man's attitude toward it. People often ask, "When is a man rich?" or "If he has such and such an amount, is he rich?" Personally, I believe Jesus was more concerned about our attitude toward money than the amount of money we have. If a man considers himself "rich," he feels above his neighbors because of his possessions. He is tempted to see them as "poor." He may show contempt for them and their rights and opinions, or even take advantage over them. On the other hand, a person may have more wealth than his neighbor, but use it as God's to bring added blessings to his church and community. As Paul says, "Some are administrators." This gift of management makes some men wealthy and enables them to help others. It is not money itself that makes it hard, or impossible, for a rich man to enter the kingdom; it is the love of money, the trust and pride in wealth, that destroys him.

Paul's Teaching About Money

In 1 Timothy 6, the Apostle Paul tells us that the love of money is a root of all kinds of evil. He says that they who would be rich fall into temptation and a snare and into many foolish and hurtful lusts. These drown men in destruction and perdition. He warns Timothy to flee from these evils, and instead to strive for what is right and good, learning to trust God and love others. When we seek wealth and things as ends in themselves, we are chasing false values. Earthly wealth is not the true value that satisfies. *True riches are righteousness, godliness, faith, love, patience, and meekness.* These are not fleeting values of the moment, but eternal values. The Scriptures exhort us to accumulate true and eternal riches and to avoid spending our lives chasing the gods of this world.

Paul also instructs "them that are rich in this world." He says riches should not become our chief goal in life. But if we become rich by hard work, wise business deals, or become heir to wealth, we should take a Christian attitude toward it. Paul does not say that it is wrong to have wealth, nor does he say that we should do away with it. Being a good steward for God does not mean that we must abandon money, but that we must strive to manage money to further God's work and help the needy.

Paul has three words of advice for the wealthy, which if obeyed will keep him from being corrupted by wealth. He must not let it "go to his head." He must not think that he is better than others because he has more money than they have. He should not make a display of his riches by expensive dress, bigger and more expensive houses or automobiles, by showy spending and big parties for other people "in his class."

Second, he must not trust in "uncertain riches," but should maintain his trust in the living God. A man of wealth is tempted to trust in his riches. He is inclined to feel that he can buy his way through life and need not depend upon God. Paul reminds us that wealth is "uncertain riches." Riches have a way of getting away from us. They cannot be depended upon. Many a man has been rich one day only to find himself bankrupt and poor the next day.

After a great fire destroyed much of Chicago years ago, three businessmen whose fortunes had been burned were discussing their losses. One man remarked, "I thank God that I put some of my money where fire could not get it." As he walked away, another said, "That man gave nearly a million dollars to the Lord's work last year. Had I not been a fool, I would have done the same."

In the third place, Paul charges the rich to use their money in doing good, to be rich in good works, ready to share with others. A person with wealth can do so much good! He can help feed the hungry, support church workers, and provide scholarships to youth preparing themselves for service. He can also give generously to promote programs of self-help in poverty areas of the world. Thank God we have people like that in our churches. Helping people is an investment that pleases God, indeed it is the only way we can give to God.

If persons with wealth do not become high-minded, do not trust in their wealth, and share generously with others, their riches will not hurt them. Persons like that will not be guilty of hoarding or of amassing excessive amounts of wealth. Rather, they will lay up treasures in heaven and be rich toward God.

We Are Stewards in Earning Money

The Christian steward will be careful how he earns his money. He will not compete unfairly. He will not take advantage of his fellowman. James says to those who have grown rich by cheating their laborers, "Listen, you rich people. Weep and howl over the miseries that shall come upon you." The prophets spoke against those who oppressed the poor and stole from them. Amos cries out against them, "Listen, you merchants who rob the poor and trample on the needy. You can hardly wait for the Sabbath and the religious holidays to end, so you can get out and start selling again. You use weighted scales

36

and undersized measures to cheat the poor. You sell worthless wheat at a high price. You find a poor man who can't pay his debts, not even a slice of bread or a pair of shoes, and buy him as a slave. The Lord has sworn, 'I won't forget your deeds.'" Tithes and offerings taken from large profits wrung from the poor will not bribe God to overlook this injustice, no matter how religious the giver tries to appear.

The Christian steward will not earn his money in a way that is hurtful to others. How can a Christian earn high wages working in a factory that manufactures ammunition and bombs that are used to kill his fellowmen? How can he earn money in making and selling alcoholic drinks and harmful drugs? Many of our highway accidents are caused by the use of alcohol, as are many of our broken homes. Hundreds of bodies and lives are destroyed annually by alcohol. Years ago a Chicago attorney declared, "Booze is the mother of crime. It drives to his deed the homicide, the stickup man, the burglar, the thief, the thug. It fires the brain of the prostitute and the beggar. I have tried an army of 50,000 [lawbreakers], most of whom were booze-soaked." Surely no responsible steward would want to earn money by making and selling alcoholic beverages at such a cost to society. The good steward of God will earn his money in pursuits that contribute to the good of his brothers and sisters.

We Are Stewards in Using Money
A. A. Hyde, a successful businessman, said that a Christian may save a modest amount for his

business and for security, but that it is sinful to accumulate for himself large amounts of money when the needs of the world are so great. He believed it was wrong for persons to save so that their children can live in luxury. He saved what was needed to carry on his business and to have modest security, but gave the remainder to worthy causes. He saved that he might be a liberal giver to the Lord's work. He gave a lot of money in his lifetime to help others.

Money can be a tremendous power in promoting the purposes of God in today's world. William Colgate had to leave home as a teenager because his parents were too poor to support him. A friend told him, "Be a good man. Give your heart to the Lord. And give Him ten cents out of every dollar you earn, and you will become a wealthy man." He followed the instruction of his friend. When he saw he was becoming wealthy, he began giving two tenths, then three, four and five tenths. Later he was giving all his net income to the Lord.

A friend of mine, whom God has prospered in a great way, once told me, "Milo, I want to die a poor man." God has entrusted him with considerable wealth. He has arranged for his family to be cared for, but in the end his possessions will go to promote worthy causes. Through the years he has been giving generously, far above 10 percent.

Should this man die today, he will die as a poor man. No money will be wasted "in settling up the estate." No family quarrels will be invited "by dividing up the inheritance."

Proper Management of Money

Earning and saving has little meaning without proper management of money. Since God gives us our possessions and holds us responsible for their management, He is concerned how we use them. The faithful steward cannot waste or squander his Lord's money. Surely he cannot use what God has entrusted to him to defeat the purposes of God. Following the pattern of the Scriptures, he will invest at least a tenth of his income in God's kingdom. The rest he must manage for his good, the good of his family and society, and for the honor of God.

One of the greatest blessings that can come from money is the blessing and joy of sharing it and using it for the building of Christ's kingdom. God's grace is necessary, even in this, for "the love of money" can trap us into acting as if we were great benefactors or philanthropists. We must also learn the "grace of giving," which we will discuss in the next chapter.

Prayer

Thank you, Lord, for entrusting to us some of Your silver and gold which can be such a tremendous blessing or curse to us and to others. May we be good stewards in using it, sharing it, and in promoting Your work on earth. Amen.

4

GENEROSITY:
PATH TO JOY

PAUL'S longest discussion of giving is found in 2 Corinthians 8 and 9. He wrote this letter to the Christians who lived in the city of Corinth. They were Greeks who became Christians through one of his earlier visits to their country. In chapter 8:1-5 he says, "Now I want to tell you what God in his grace has done for the churches in Macedonia. Though they have been going through much trouble and hard times, they have mixed their wonderful joy with their deep poverty, and the result has been an overflow of giving to others. They gave not only what they could afford, but far more; and I can testify that they did it because they wanted to, and not because of nagging on my part. They begged us to take the money so they could share in the joy of helping the Christians in Jerusalem. Best of all, they went beyond our highest hopes, for their first action was to dedicate themselves to the Lord and to us, for whatever directions God might give to them through us" *(Living Bible)*.

Though these Macedonian Christians were poor, they gave liberally to help Jewish Christians they had never met. "They begged us to take the money so they could share in the joy of helping the Christians in Jerusalem." Paul calls this spirit "the grace of God bestowed on the churches of Macedonia." The desire and the joy of giving is a grace from God. Paul told the Christians in Corinth, "See that you excel in this gracious work also" (2 Corinthians 8:7).

The Way to Happy Living

In Palestine there are two seas fed by the river Jordan. The Sea of Galilee abounds with fish and life. Its waters are fresh, for water flows in, and water flows out. It not only receives, but gives out also. Some miles down the Jordan River is the Dead Sea in which no fish or plants can live. It receives water from the Jordan just as does the Sea of Galilee, but it has no outlet. The sun dries up the water, and the sea keeps all the minerals the river carries in. So the sea becomes ever more bitter and salty. Unless one wants to be like the Dead Sea, he must give out as well as take in.

The noted missionary and evangelist E. Stanley Jones has said, "It cannot be insisted too much that abundant living means abundant giving. You are made that way in every structure of your being. If you only breathed in and refused to breath out, you would smother yourself to death. In a similar way, if you are not outgoing, the whole process of incoming will stop and you will die spiritually and physically. If a cow is not milked, it will go dry. If you are not giving out to others, you, too, will go dry in spirit.''

Some Modern Illustrations

A leader in a Mennonite congregation in Ghana began to give regularly. His example is an encouragement to others. His willingness to give has opened his life to further growth. Christ now has greater access to his life and through him is able to bless the people of his congregation.

A pastor in Kansas became concerned about the laxness of his members in giving and in living. The church was not meeting its honest debts. This pastor began giving messages on biblical stewardship, to which his people responded. The giving of the congregation increased and there was a corresponding spiritual renewal. Members were added to the church and the young people received new life.

Adolfo Torres in Belize began working for the Mennonite Center store in Orange Walk Town about five years ago. Gradually he worked his way up to manager and in July 1977 bought the store. One of his first acts was to set up a donations account into which he carefully puts at least 10 percent of the net profit each month for the Lord's work. On one occasion when there were unusual expenses, someone suggested that he skip the donation for that month and give more later. But he refused saying, "The Lord's portion comes first." The business is growing nicely and each month there has been a profit.

Why Should We Give Generously?

Why should Christians give generously of themselves, their talents, and their possessions?

1. God loves a cheerful giver. Generous gifts are "an order of a sweet smell, a sacrifice acceptable, well-pleasing to God." "It is more blessed to give than to receive."

2. The Scriptures urge us to give a portion to the Lord. Whenever God asks us to give, it is for our good. God told Israel to tithe so that "your God may bless you in all the work of your hands."

In Proverbs we read, "Honor the Lord by giving him the first part of all your income, and he will fill your barns with wheat and barley and overflow your wine vats with the finest wines" (*Living Bible*).

God says, through the prophet Malachi, "Bring all the tithes into the storehouse . . . [and] I will open up the windows of heaven and pour you out a blessing." Our Lord said, "Give, and it will be given to you; good measure, pressed down, shaken together, running over."

3. Our gratitude for what we have received can be expressed by the way we give. "Freely ye have received, freely give." We have received so much from God and others that we should want to give to others.

4. The Scriptures point out the blessing and joy of giving, for joy and giving are closely related. In 1 Chronicles 29 David called his people together and told them of his plan for building a house of God. He himself gave thousands of talents of silver and gold. (One talent equals 75 pounds or 34 kilograms.) He challenged his officers and leaders to give. They, too, gave thousands of talents of gold, silver, brass, and iron. Then "the people rejoiced because with a willing heart they offered willingly to the Lord, and David also rejoiced with great joy."

We notice also in Acts 2 and 4 that when the Spirit came upon the believers at Jerusalem none of them called their possessions their own, but they sold their property and laid the income at the apostles' feet. "And great grace was upon them all." They "did eat their meat with gladness and singleness of heart, praising God." Grace, joy, and gladness accompanied generous giving.

5. Our love and compassion compels us to give. If we see our brother in need and shut up our heart of compassion, how does the love of God dwell in us? "The love of Christ constrains us." When millions have never heard the gospel and thousands are in poverty, how can I be a true follower of Christ and not respond as I am able?

How Much Should I Give?

After Paul had told the Corinthians to give for the needs of Christians at Jerusalem, he added, "Each person must make up his mind what he will give. He must not be pushed or compelled to give. God loves the man who is happy when he gives. But do not let fear of the future prevent you from being generous.''

But how do I make up my mind what to give? Do I give what is left over after I have everything I want? Do I compare what others give? Do I look at what the Scriptures teach? Israel was asked to give tithes of their crops and of their flocks. Would that be the standard for Christians? Many have been greatly blessed by setting aside a tenth for the Lord. The churches that stress this kind of giving are among the churches with the highest per person giving.

Tithing may mean a real, but rewarding, sacrifice for new Christians. Many Christians in more prosperous communities believe the tithe is not nearly enough. I know of a doctor who is giving 50 percent of his income to the needy and to the church. I know of a prosperous businessman who gives 40 percent of his income. Others are giving 25 percent.

A. A. Hyde, the maker of Mentholatum, believed that tithing is for the poor and for those of moderate circumstances. He felt that a prosperous man should give beyond 10 percent. Can any Christian with an annual income far above his needs be content to give only a tithe? Or how can a wealthy Christian be content to let the low-income wage earner suffer? The New Testament instructs us to give as God prospers, or in proportion to what He gives us.

Where Should We Give Our Money?
In some areas of the world, such as North

America, one may receive many requests for funds. In the United States one even finds dishonest fund raisers who thrive on "charitable contributions" and misuse the money given to them by well-meaning Christians. So how do I decide what cause to support?

Each Christian should endeavor to do his full share in supporting his local church. Since he enjoys the benefits of the church, he should do what he can to support it.

He also should be interested in supporting the work of the churches in his area. This work of the larger church—at home and abroad—includes hospitals and clinics, schools and colleges, starting new churches, and producing nurture and witness materials.

Each Christian should, like the Macedonians, be concerned about the needs of others. Every individual, congregation, and conference should do its share, if possible, to carry the gospel to other parts of the world.

Each of us will want to support the various ministries of our church. I believe the Mennonite Church has a sound biblical program and needs all the money, talents, and energy I can contribute. I believe my church handles my funds efficiently and wisely. I do not feel guilty ignoring appeals from other religious groups because I give generously to my own church.

I suggest that you be careful about responding to financial appeals from other religious groups. One man with a worldwide program, who appears on TV and radio, makes a strong appeal for money. Although he receives thousands of dollars from viewers and listeners, I believe he is teaching false doctrines. Other fund raisers spend only about 10 percent of the money raised for the cause they represent. Why, then, should I respond to such fund raisers when my denomination has a worthy program? If I am convinced that my church is obeying God, I will think first of helping carry on its work.

The Biblical Program of My Church

I believe the ministries of the Mennonite Church are firmly based on the Scriptures. By supporting the Mennonite Church, I can have a part in establishing churches in other lands. I can send relief to needy persons around the world. I can help support those who are working in agriculture, medicine, education, literature, etc. I can help people in poverty areas of the world to help themselves. I can have a part in building colleges, hospitals, youth camps, nursing homes, and in releasing gospel radio programs to many countries. I can help victims of floods, tornadoes, earthquakes, and other natural disasters.

What a privilege! What a challenge to give generously to promote these causes! How wonderful to be a partner of God in promoting His purposes around the world. I can have a part in extending His kingdom everywhere.

Prayer

Thank you, Lord, that while You were rich You became poor for our sakes. Help us to give generously of ourselves and of our possessions that others may be rich in Thee. Amen.

5

THE MARKS
OF A WISE
STEWARD

A poor widow in India could hardly support her children, but when the day came to dedicate a church building, she was there.

Another woman present in the congregation, who had more of this world's goods, thought, "I would like to give something in this offering this morning, but I have nothing."

When the offering was taken, the people went forward to place their gifts in a basket. To the amazement of the wealthier woman, the poor widow, with face beaming, placed one whole rupee in the offering basket. At that time, a rupee would have bought much for her children. But she was happy to be able to give her one rupee. The wealthier woman felt ashamed of herself, because she thought she had nothing to give.°

God wants to meet the needs of others through His people. But He can do this only if His people are responsible stewards, as was the Indian widow. So if our neighbors starve, if our evangelists are not paid, it is not because God is too poor to meet their needs. Rather, it will be because we have been careless stewards. Let each of us ask, "How can I be a responsible steward?"

The Marks of a Responsible Steward

Like the Macedonians, I will first give myself to the Lord. When I believe in my heart and confess with my lips that Jesus is Lord, I become an open channel for Him. As a member of His body, the church, I will be a responsible steward.

As a responsible steward, I will use the resources at my disposal to develop a strong body, mind, personality, and character so I can be the temple of God and better serve others.

I will recognize that all I am and have belongs to God. I am but a trustee, a steward, of all that God has entrusted to me. I am responsible for its proper use and must give account before God as to how I use it. I will give as the Lord blesses me and help as the Spirit and the church direct.

I will faithfully and loyally support the work of

°From The Foundation Series story collection, used by permission of The Foundation Series Publishing Council, Nappanee, Indiana; Newton, Kansas; Scottdale, Pennsylvania.

His church. As we promote the work of the church, we promote our Lord's work. This must be so if the church is truly the body of Christ.

As a responsible steward, I will use my talents, as well as my possessions, for the good of the body of Christ. I can do this by teaching in the Bible or Sunday school, serving on a committee, assisting in the upkeep of the church building, and the like.

Since I enjoy fellowship with Christ and the church, I will want others to enjoy these same privileges. Therefore, I will be interested in bringing others to faith in God and into the fellowship of the church.

As a responsible steward, I will share the compassion of the Lord for the poor, the sick, and the downtrodden. My caring for all the people God has created shows my love for the Lord Himself.

I will use time wisely, for time is a precious trust from God. I will use it to improve my character and personality. I will use it to serve mankind and God. I will keep one day of the week for worship and witness, rest and relaxation, and use some time each day for Bible study, meditation, and prayer. I will take time for fellowship, worship, and recreation with my family. I will spend time with people.

I will remember God created a good earth, with good soil, good water, good atmosphere, good vegetation, and good creatures. After each creative act God said "that it was good." He said, "Let us make man . . . and let them have dominion." Man was to be caretaker. I will, therefore, try to be a wise "earth-keeper."

Ways to Be Wise Earth-Keepers

Realize that the earth is the Lord's. God is concerned not only for man, but also for His creation. He wants to reconcile all of creation, including man, to Himself. Thus, we will work to fulfill His purposes.

Put stewardship of creation above gain for ourselves. We want clean environment, pure water and atmosphere, but tend to neglect these when they keep us from making money.

Choose a manner of life pleasing to God and do not follow the world's patterns.

Seek contentment and godliness rather than earthly comfort and security. For example, we will buy what is necessary and not what advertisers say we need.

Make this earth what God wants it to be. We will care about how the soil, the forests, and the natural resources are used. We will use fuel sparingly. We will be interested in developing new sources of energy. We will do our part to keep the air, the water, and the earth clean.

Charles B. Shenk, Mennonite board of Missions worker in Japan, reports how a family in the Nakashibetsu congregation is trying to be good stewards. Dairy farming, the major industry in the area in which they live, is becoming highly specialized. The general trend is to increase production by every means possible: by buying more and larger equipment, by pouring heavier doses of chemical fertilizers on small pieces of land, by putting more minerals and food concentrate into overworked cows and more work onto overworked laborers.

This brother has been saying for years, "I refuse, as a Christian, to get caught in that rat race." And he is living what he believes. Rather than push the land, the cows, or the laborers "to give everything they've got" (100 percent), he says, "I'll settle for 80 percent all around. I might not get rich, and that doesn't matter. But perhaps I can save my land from exhaustion, my cattle from dropping dead, and have more time for my family and the Lord's work."

Shenk comments, "My observation is that after three years or more of experience, he is proving his point. And as an extra benefit, he's having a lot of fun doing it. Further, my family and I, the pastor, and others in the congregation are the grateful recipients of fresh milk free from his farm. This brother and sister have been a real inspiration to us, not just for what they believe, but the way they practice it with joy."

As responsible stewards, we will dedicate our time, talents, and possessions to help people to be the persons God wants them to be and to help make the earth the good place God wants it to be for His people.

Prayer
Thank you again, Lord, for permitting us to be Your stewards. Forgive us where we have failed to be faithful. Help us to be responsible stewards of Yours. Amen.

6

ENCOURAGE
GENEROUS
GIVING

THE great needs of the people of the world call
for generous giving by God's people. The twin
tasks of evangelizing and feeding the world are
being hindered by lack of funds. Yet many
members in our churches in North America give
only 5 percent or less of their income. As a result,
thousands of people will never hear the gospel
and thousands more will perish by starvation.
And God's people are deprived of the joy and
rich blessings God has promised, and longs to
give, to generous stewards.

God, in His Word, asks His people to give, and
what He asks of us is always for our good. We are

the losers if we disobey. Paul exhorts us to give liberally because we will then reap bountifully. He says giving brings glory to God, produces an outpouring of praises to God, and proves that our religion is real (2 Corinthians 9:12-14, Laubach).

The great needs of people of the world compel us to give. If we have of this world's goods, but are unconcerned about the suffering and poverty of others, how does God's love dwell in us? If we fail to give, we hinder the spread of the gospel. I served on the executive committee of the Mennonite Board of Missions for a number of years. Sometimes when new areas opened for a Christian witness, the Board had no funds to start another work. The building of His kingdom was being hindered.

Spiritual blessings result from generous giving. Our generous support for God's work will also increase our interest in God's kingdom. "Where your treasure is, your heart will be." Generous giving enriches life—"There is no abundant living without abundant giving." Life becomes more meaningful as we give ourselves and our possessions to promote the worthy purposes of God. Generous giving can save us from the cancer of covetousness and materialism which can destroy us. Generous sharing helps resolve the problems of human relationships. It will help remove tensions between the rich and the poor around the world. Certainly these are worthy motivations for generous giving.

Ways to Encourage Generous Giving
Paul tells us that the Macedonians gave be-

yond their ability because they had received the grace of God. If God's people are filled with His love, His compassion, and His Spirit, they will gladly give. If I am able, but unwilling, to give generously, I have failed to receive God's rich gifts. When the Holy Spirit was poured out upon the believers in Jerusalem, great grace was upon them all, and they gave generously (Acts 4:33, 34). One way to encourage generous giving is to help other believers to receive and experience more fully God's grace.

Giving is a part of total stewardship—an important part of stewardship of the gospel. We are partners of God, receiving all we have from Him and using it to promote His cause. We dedicate our bodies, minds, talents, and possessions to minister to others. Stewardship of money makes sense only as a part of total stewardship, total commitment. Encourage other Christians to commit all of life to the lordship of Christ. This will help make more money and other material resources available for the building of Christ's kingdom.

We must help each other to be aware of the great needs of the world. People who are not informed of needs will be less likely to give to meet those needs. People must constantly be reminded that giving to the church is giving to people, meeting the needs of people, promoting the purposes of God. People also want to know where their money is being spent and what it is doing. They must be kept informed of the work of their church and its various agencies and institutions.

Congregational leaders need to encourage and

challenge their members to give. These leaders should never beg, threaten, or scold their people. This will not promote genuine Christian stewardship. Like Paul in 2 Corinthians 8 and 9, leaders must inform their people of the need, and challenge them to respond. Leaders can cite examples of generous giving, and praise people when they respond. Leaders should be an example to the congregation of generous giving. Pastors, treasurers, and other congregational leaders who are not cheerful givers are not likely to develop a giving church.

Giving is based in the very nature of God and in people made in God's image. Giving is a fundamental principle in the teaching of the Scriptures. Faithful men of God were generous givers. The principle of tithing was taught in the Old Testament and practiced by the faithful. Giving as God prospered is taught in the New Testament. Churches that teach and emphasize giving usually have the best records in giving. Many people have been richly blessed by giving 10 percent or more of their income.

Special needs can also stimulate giving. These might include helping a brother or sister with a hospital bill, providing food for a starving family, or starting a new congregation. Our church hospitals, schools, mission committees, publication boards, and other agencies always have special needs you can support. Congregational leaders may fear that these special projects will lessen the giving for the local church. I believe these generally increase giving. Pastors, teachers, and other congregational leaders should be alert to opportunities to challenge their members to give. Giving regularly to the local church and, when needed, to special projects is a good practice.

Examples of Increased Giving

One congregation that was weak in giving came to the end of the year with many unpaid bills. With the counsel of the congregation, the pastor decided to have a "Prove the Tithe Month." Each member was to give a tenth of his weekly income for the month. At the end of the month the congregation had raised more money than it needed to pay outstanding bills. Some of the members were so blessed by the experience that they continued to tithe their income.

Another pastor was called to a church that was giving very little to missions. He was deeply concerned about his people and their stewardship of the gospel. He knew that his church contained weak Christians who had little joy in their lives. It also contained strong Christians whose joy was deep and genuine. He knew that the difference lay in their attitude toward money. He preached messages on Christian commitment and the joy of sharing and urged that 50 percent of the giving go for missions. The results were astounding.

In three years, the giving for missions increased more than 300 percent. The giving for the local church increased also. But more important, people found new joy in their lives. One member declared, "I used to give little and it hurt. Now I give a lot and it is the greatest pleasure I have in life." Other churches followed their example and increased their giving, as well as their spiritual life.

A large church had no pastor for some months. Their giving went down as well as their interest in the church's program. Near the close of the year, there was a large deficit in the treasury. They called a pastor who began to emphasize biblical stewardship. Before each offering he read a verse or two of Scripture, pointed out the joy of giving, and expressed appreciation for the response of his people. He suggested that if each member would increase his giving 25 percent, the deficit could be erased by the end of the year. He promised to increase his own giving by this amount. His members accepted the challenge. The deficit was more than met and the congregation rejoiced.

Another pastor felt his people were not giving nearly their full potential and were missing a blessing. He called a special speaker to teach stewardship for one week. They announced at the start of the meetings that an offering for missions would be taken the last evening of the meetings. In response to this challenge, the congregation gave more than $6,000 for missions. Because of this emphasis, the pastor reported that one year later the giving of the congregation had increased considerably.

We must help people see the relationship between faith and giving. Lack of faith often keeps people from giving. They are afraid God's promises may fail. Paul tells the Corinthians, "But do not let fear of the future prevent you from being generous. God is able to bless you with more than you need. He will give you so much that you will always be able to give to every good cause" (2 Corinthians 9:8, Laubach).

Satan often tries to keep people from giving by suggesting, "You can't afford to give a tithe of your income." Or, "You won't be able to pay your bills if you give generously." Giving is often a test of faith. Do we really believe that it is more blessed to give than to receive? Do we believe that if we seek first the kingdom, other things will be added to us? Helping believers to increase their faith in God will likely lead to increased giving.

Some time ago, I knew of an urgent need in a Christian family and felt God wanted to help meet that need through me. But the thought came, "You can't help them. Your taxes are due next week. You will need several hundred dollars to meet another need." But I brushed the thought aside and did what I believed God was asking me to do. I sent them a check, believing it would not really affect my bank account. God was wanting to channel some of His wealth through me. A few days later, we received a check we were not expecting—much larger than the one I had sent. I felt a bit guilty. Perhaps God wanted to help that family in a greater way, but my faith was too small.

God wants to meet the needs of His people and the needs of the church by channeling His riches through us. To be His faithful stewards means we give generously, not what is ours, but what is His. How wonderful to be channels through which the riches of God flow to bless the needy of the world and to promote the work of His church.

Finally, we must encourage the stewardship of accumulated wealth. In Luke 12 we have the story of a man who was not a good steward of accumulated wealth. God had given him large crops so that he did not have room to store all his goods. He, therefore, built larger barns in which to hoard them. But just as he had amassed this great wealth, God called him from this world and asked, "Now whose things shall these things be that you have accumulated?" God called him a fool. Why was he a fool?

First, he failed to recognize God's ownership. He spoke of "My barns, my goods, my fruit, my soul." He failed to see that these were but trusts from God to be shared and used for the promotion of the kingdom.

Second, he was making a foolish investment—storing up treasures on the earth where he was sure to lose them. They could have become treasures laid up in heaven.

Third, he was foolish because he overlooked the fact that he would have to give an account before God of how he had used his gifts. Daniel Webster was once asked to share the most serious thought that ever entered his mind. He answered, "My accountability to God."

Fourth, the rich fool was unfair to God and his fellowmen. Without the help of God, he never could have been rich. If society had not provided a market, his goods would have been worthless. Had he been thankful and wise, he would have shared.

Fifth, he was foolish because he overlooked the

60

blessing his wealth could have been if properly shared. He missed the joy of feeding the hungry, ministering to the needy, and promoting the purposes of God.

Jesus said, "So is he who lays up treasure for himself, and is not rich toward God." Would Jesus call some of us foolish? Let us avoid the pitfall of laying up treasure in the earth instead of wisely investing it in the kingdom. It is not enough to merely give tithes of our income, we are trustees also of accumulated wealth.

How sad when God entrusts a person with wealth and he merely stores it up where it does no one any good, and he loses it in the end. A good steward will plan for his possessions to serve worthy purposes after his death. In this plan or "will," he will remember the Lord who gave him all that he has.

Some people name their congregation or a church agency, such as Mennonite Board of Missions, to share with the other heirs of their will. Think of all the good that could be done if everyone with wealth would do that. A good steward will want his possessions serving the Lord after he dies.

"Eye hath not seen, nor ear heard, neither have entered into the heart of man, the things which God hath prepared for them that love him" (1 Corinthians 2:9). How rewarding to be a faithful steward of God! Notice the rewards of two faithful stewards in Matthew 25 as they give account to their Lord. First, the praise of the master: "Well done, good and faithful servant." Second, promotion: "You have been faithful over a little, I will set you over much." Third, sharing the glory of their Master: "Enter into the joy of your master."

Prayer

Thank you, Lord, for the privilege of studying the doctrine of Christian stewardship. Help us realize more fully the joys and rewards of faithful stewardship and the penalties for unfaithfulness. Grant that we always may be Your responsible stewards. Amen.

FOR FURTHER READING AND STUDY

Helen Alderfer, Editor, *A Farthing in Her Hand*, Herald Press, 1964.

Wallace E. Fisher. *A New Climate for Stewardship*, Abingdon Press, 1976.

Robert J. Hastings. *My Money and My God*, Broadman Press, 1961.

C. W. Hatch. *Stewardship Enriches Life*, Warner Press, 1951.

Milo Kauffman. *Stewards of God*, Herald Press, 1975.

A. Grace Wenger. *Stewards of the Gospel*, Herald Press, 1964.

Milo Kauffman, Hesston, Kansas, grew to manhood on a farm in North Dakota. He received his high school and college training at Hesston College. While a student at the college he was ordained to the ministry in December 1924 to serve a mission church near Peabody, Kansas. Having been asked to serve on the Bible faculty at Hesston, he went to Chicago for seminary training. He received his BD from Northern Baptist Seminary and his MA in Religious Education at McCormick Theological Seminary.

After graduation from seminary, he spent about eighteen months in evangelistic work throughout the church before accepting the call to become president of Hesston College. He served in this position for nineteen years (1932-1951). Since that time he has been engaged as evangelist, writer, lecturer, pastor, and teacher.

During much of this time he has been associated with Hesston College. At present he is serving the college half time in church relations and is available to churches for stewardship conferences and other types of meetings.

He is the author of *Personal Work* (1940), *The Challenge of Christian Stewardship* (1955), and *Stewards of God* (1975). The two former books went through five printings each. He also has served widely on church boards and committees. He was moderator of the South Central Conference and of the Mennonite Church.